Introduction

If there is one small animal that conjures up an unsavory image in the minds of most people, it is the common house rat. Mere mention of its name is enough to send shivers down the spine of most moms. To actually see one usually changes the shivers to horror! The rat has a general popularity on par with a tarantula or a snake. Is this image based on reality or on myth? The fact is, the rat is a much-maligned animal, just as the other two creatures are. Its reputation is based on hard facts, but these facts have been twisted and used over the years in order to paint a frightening picture of what is a potentially very endearing little pet.

At once, you must make a distinction between the common wild rat and the fancy variety that is gaining popularity as a pet. They are as different as chalk and cheese in many ways, though, of course, they are anatomically one and the same. You may be aware that the black rat, *Rattus rattus*, was the carrier of the deadly bubonic plague that was known as the Black Death in Medieval Europe. It killed millions of people there, and in other parts of the world. The brown, or Norway, rat, *Rattus norvegicus*, is the creature that you are most likely to see scurrying around old warehouses, barns, cellars, and sewers.

This hardly seems a rosy image of these delightful little pets! But let us stand back and cast aside the images created by Hollywood movie makers, who always portray the rat in its worst possible light, and view the rat as just

◆ Fancy rats come in a wide range of color patterns that are not seen in wild specimens.

◆ This pet rat displays the alertness typical of its species. When a rat stands on its hind legs, which it does quite frequently, it uses its tail for balance.

1

▲ Originally, rats made their way to the New World via ships, often climbing the ropes like this nimble fellow.

another small animal. It is highly intelligent and extremely adaptable to many environments. It displays a high level of sociability; and while it has caused the deaths of millions of people, it has also saved as many in its role as a laboratory specimen.

Its basic attributes are much the same as those of a dog or a cat, but in a smaller package. Its evil reputation, if you wish to get down to the nitty gritty of the matter, is the direct result of us humans creating garbage, filth, and squalor on an enormous scale. Rats, like the mouse and many other creatures, have merely capitalized on what to them is a food source and a means of surviving in a hard world. Remove those elements from the equation and you have a furry animal that is basically no different from a squirrel, mouse, hamster, gerbil, guinea pig, or chinchilla.

Each of these animals is related. They are zoologically classified in the mammalian order known as Rodentia—the rodents. This is by far the largest mammalian order, the rodents accounting for 41 percent of all mammals, while the rat and its family relatives account for 63 percent of all rodents. Rabbits, which many people think are rodents, are not. They are in a related order called Lagomorpha. The Norway rat, which is the one pets were mainly bred from, hails from Asia and probably arrived in Europe during the 1550s on trading ships. It is thought to have made its debut in the USA about 1775, also via sailing ships. In Europe, it displaced the black rat, which preferred a more arboreal existence in roofs and was more readily removed by humans with the passage of years.

The main reason why rats, and to a lesser extent mice, have gained an unsavory reputation is that they, more than any other rodents, have chosen to live in and around human settlements. They have done so since the first formation of these settlements, in the days of the early Egyptians. However, of the very many rat and mouse species, only a small handful have chosen to live near humans.

This rat has been allowed out of its cage for exercise. If you are going to let your pet out of its cage, be sure to stay close by to supervise him.

The Fancy Rat

You must make a mental distinction between the wild rats and the ones you may choose to keep as pets. Although the wild rat may indeed have been caught and reared as a sort of pet centuries ago, it was not until the 19th century that the "fancy rat" hobby began. It is probable that it derived from two sources. First, large numbers of rats were captured so they could be released into the rat pens used for the pastime of rat killing by dogs, usually terriers. Second, rats became (and remain) subjects for experimental work by doctors and scientists.

From scientists, in the main, the pet rats were bred. Given the numbers of laboratory rats produced, which has run into many millions, it is not surprising that color mutations occurred. They provided much impetus to the hobby, as they do in all other pet species. These fancy rats were thus not your everyday house types but specimens that were free of carrying the very diseases that have been the plague of humans for centuries.

In the course of their captive breeding, over hundreds of generations, they have become more docile than their wild brethren.

A rat's vibrissae, or whiskers, act as sensory devices as the animal moves about in its surroundings.

3

An aquarium tank can make an ideal home for a pet rat. Just make sure to equip it with a secure, well-ventilated lid.

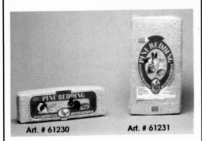

Art. # 61230   Art. # 61231

Pet shops stock a wide variety of floor covering materials that are suitable for rats. Photo courtesy Rolf C. Hagen Corp.

Absorbency is an important factor to consider when selecting your rat's floor covering and bedding. Photo courtesy Rolf C. Hagen Corp.

Accommodations

When keeping any pet animal, its housing needs are extremely important. You need to provide sufficient space in which it can live, provide security so that it cannot escape, and ensure that the accommodations are made of materials that are readily cleaned so they stay in a germ-free condition. For rodents, bearing in mind their capacity to render wood into matchsticks, the choice for housing materials is restricted to metal or glass. Fiberglass and other plastics are no better than wood where rats are concerned, because these pets can easily bite through these materials.

The Best Housing Choice

Commercial mouse cages are much too small for rats, the same being true of hamster cages. By far the best choice would be a large glass aquarium or one made of very strong thermoplastic that is molded or framed so that there are no exposed edges—on which the pet can gnaw. The top of the aquarium should be covered with either metal gauze or finch-size cage front bars, which are small enough to prevent escape. For aesthetic effect, you could then cover the top with an aquarium hood equipped with blue-fluorescent lights.

House Size

The size of your pet's house is, of course, a very subjective matter, but even so you should work on the premise that the larger it is the better. It makes management easier and allows your pet far more room to move around in a natural manner. You also have much more scope for decoration in a large unit. This being so, a size of 24x12x15 in. (62x31x38cm) may be regarded as a minimum. Some might say this is large, but in my experience many hobbyists skimp on accommodations to the detriment of their pets.

Another point you should bear in mind is that your rat's house can be expanded. With a little imagination, you can develop a super complex. For example, if you were to obtain (at a later date) another aquarium, you could connect the two via a metal or thermoplastic tube. This is easier if your tanks are themselves thermoplastic. The result is two living areas that can be decorated in a different manner. Even with a single unit, you can fashion a platform that creates a second living level, possibly as the sleeping area—or maybe this could be the main feeding area.

Floor Covering

The floor of the accommodations should be kind to your pet's feet, yet capable of absorbing urine. With this in mind, some suitable choices are sawdust (the kind sold for pets, as it will not have been treated with potentially toxic chemicals), granulated paper that is specially formulated for small rodents, and natural plant litter. Natural plant litter is gaining popularity with cat owners as being a far better litter than the traditional clay/grit types. (This new litter is produced from crushed grasses and bits of wood that are left over after logging operations).

The base substrate can then be covered with wood shavings or hay. Hay will also be used as a food item, as might the natural plant litter just discussed. Hay or shredded paper will make the best nesting material, or you can use any of the commercial nesting materials produced for rodents. Avoid the use of nylon in any form, or

◆ This shed rattery has been designed to comfortably accommodate a large number of rats. It is roomy, well-ventilated, and secure from predators.

◆ A good investment for the pet-rat owner is a small-animal carrying case such as the one shown here. It will make transporting your pet a breeze. Photo courtesy Rolf C. Hagen Corp.

Cages for rats and other small mammals are available in a number of functional, attractive styles. Photo courtesy Rolf C. Hagen Corp.

the wood-like string used in packing cases. This can get entangled around the neck of young rats, or could prove dangerous if swallowed. Sand is very abrasive, while soil carries the risk of introducing pathogens (disease-causing organisms) into the accommodations.

Decoration and Toys

Rats are extremely intelligent animals and will appreciate consideration of this fact. This apart, you as well as they will enjoy aesthetically pleasing housing. You could include a few large smooth pebbles or pieces of granite of varying sizes in one area of the home. These objects are easily cleaned. Log branches can also be a feature of the home. They, together with the pebbles, can be used to create interesting little hiding places. Slate is another

If you wish to keep a pair of rats, it is best to choose females. Young males can get along together, but once they reach maturity, there is a strong possibility of aggressive behavior toward one another.

useful material for creating a little tunnel effect, as is piping that has been "camouflaged." With a little ingenuity, you can create a very natural–looking effect—why have a boring setup? Be sure to allow plenty of free running room in your pet's home.

Wheels of suitable size will be good exercise toys for your pet. They should be of the wooden type so that your pet's tail cannot get caught between the bars, as might happen with those made of wire. Cardboard tubes, wooden spools, and twigs are other no-cost items that your pet will play with and destroy, but they are easily replaced. The actual sleeping quarters should be comprised of a box structure of about 6 in. (15cm) cubed. It should be of stout

← Rats love to climb. This pink-eyed white is enjoying climbing around on a piece of natural untreated wood.

↑ Some rat hobbyists provide their pets with toys made of wood. This is fine, but remember that toys of this type are subject to a rat's gnawing and may have to be replaced periodically. Additionally, keep in mind that wooden toys are not moisture resistant and can absorb urine.

▲ An alert young rat peering out from his cosy hideaway. Young rats especially enjoy playthings in which they can tunnel in and out.

construction so that it will not be readily gnawed. It can be at floor level, raised on legs, or a platform approached via a wooden slatted ladder.

House Placement

The housing unit should be placed at a convenient height, both to make viewing easy for you, and so that you do not have to bend in order to attend to cleaning chores. It is very important that it is not placed in such a way that it is exposed to the fierce rays of the sun. Otherwise your pet will become stressed from excessive heat. Rats are essentially crepuscular (twilight) and nocturnal (nighttime) creatures in their habits. This is why blue lighting tubes are handy: you can watch your pet move about when the room is dark. Of course, your pet will become familiar with being handled during the hours of daylight.

The normal temperature range within the average home will be fine for your pet as long as it has cozy bedding material in which it can keep warm overnight during the colder months. This is especially important if you keep your rat in unheated outdoor accommodations, such as a shed. If your pet's housing incorporates a wire cage front, be sure it is not placed where it might be subjected to drafts, such as near a window or opposite a door. Additionally, it should not be placed immediately next to, or over, heating units. Your pet can cope adequately with most temperatures but will suffer badly if it is subject to rapid changes.

◀ These rats' sleeping quarters have been fashioned from a plastic milk container. The basic care of rats is fairly simple.

Choosing a Rat

Rats are not especially long-lived animals. Their average life expectancy is on the order of two to three years, though a well-cared-for individual may attain four or more years. With this in mind, it is obviously best to obtain a youngster. A further advantage of a young specimen is that it can more readily be hand tamed. Young rats are weaned from their mother's milk by the time they are about three weeks old, and they will have started eating solid foods at the age of 10 to 12 days. This means that a good time to obtain your new pet will be when it is about four weeks old.

Initial Considerations

Before you rush out and buy a young rat, you should consider what your needs are. Is it required purely as a pet, or might you want to exhibit it? Is there the possibility you may wish to use it for breeding? These aspects, and the matters of which sex and which colors are preferred, are best dealt with in advance so you do not waste your money and time on one or

◆ Before selecting a rat, you should first decide what your needs are. Do you want solely a pet, an exhibition-quality animal, or one that would be good for breeding? These factors should be carefully considered before you make your final decision.

◆ This pair of pet rats is perfectly happy to travel around on their owner's shoulder.

◆ Rats are hardy, interesting little creatures that can make good pets and can be a source of true pleasure.

◆ Rats can make good pets for people of all ages. The more time and attention you devote to your pet, the more accustomed it will become to be being handled.

more individuals that may not meet your specific needs. Regardless of the quality of your new pet, it must be a healthy example. Otherwise, your money really will have been wasted. Finally, whatever your choice, it is always best to have your pet's accommodations ready in advance.

Pet, Show, or Breeding Stock?

A pet-quality rat does not mean an inferior individual but rather one that displays one or more faults that would make it unsuitable for exhibition. Maybe its color or pattern is not as dense or well marked as it should be. It may be long snouted, not well balanced in its general conformation, or it may have a poor tail. However, none of these things will affect its potential as a pet. A pet-quality rat will be the most easily obtainable individual and also the least costly.

● This type of exercise wheel is not recommended for a rat, as the animal's tail can easily get caught in the spokes and be injured. If you want to provide an exercise wheel, be sure to select one with an enclosed back.

The exhibition rat will range from sound to superb in its color, pattern (if applicable), and structure. Ideally, it will be a young adult so that its full potential is apparent rather than hoped for. You might obtain a youngster that has already won some awards. This rat will be more costly, given that no rats are expensive when compared with, say, a dog or a cat.

The breeding-quality rat may not actually be up to show quality, though normally it will be. The main points about breeding stock are that its qualities are known for sure. Breeding stock is best obtained from a person who has kept detailed records of his program, and whose "type" quality is consistent. The cost of such stock will be more expensive than that of pet examples, just how much more being dependent on how well known and respected its breeder is. Mature proven breeders will be more costly than unproven stock from the same source.

▲ Choose a rat that is bright eyed, alert, and nicely furred, with no bald patches.

Colors and Patterns

Colors and patterns are very much matters of individual preference. What appeals to you may not do so to others. Some colors are more popular than others, the same being true of

▼ An agouti hooded rat. Its markings are fairly even in their distribution.

▼ Black-eyed white rex.

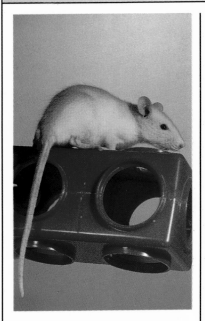

→ Pink-eyed white. When buying toys that have openings in them, be sure the openings are large for your pet to fit through with ease.

→ A blue rat. This is one of the newer color varieties to emerge from the rat hobby.

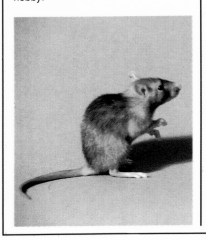

patterns. Here it need only be said that you should not allow yourself to be sold a rat that you really do not want. If you want a hooded pattern, then do not settle for a self (single)-colored individual. With patience, you will locate the exact color and pattern that you want.

The Matter of Gender

From a pet perspective, it really isn't important which sex your rat is. Both are delightful. The male may tend to have a

→ Capped rats have color only on their heads. This is a mink capped rat.

characteristic odor, but even this depends on just how well you attend cleaning chores—it certainly isn't in any way offensive. If you wish to keep two or more rats together, then always choose females, as they get along with each other much better than do males. Males may be kept with each other while they are young; but once they mature, or have scented a female, or been with one, they will thereafter tend to be very aggressive with their own sex.

The size of the accommodations is also vital when two males, and even females, are kept together. When any animal (including humans!) has insufficient living space around it, free from intrusion by its own kind, tempers will start to fray and fighting may occur.

I advise you to never keep a male and female together, other than for specific breeding purposes. If you do, you will have to contend with litter after litter of babies. Rats are prolific breeders. You might find it all but impossible to locate homes for the youngsters, and they will quickly need their own accommodations. Matters may then soon get really out of hand, so do not let the situation start in the first place.

→ An agouti rat. This coloration is created by bands of brown and black on the hair shafts.

Selecting a Healthy Individual

Purchase your new pet only from a seller whose stock is kept in very clean housing that is not overcrowded. This way, you increase the chances that your pet will be healthy. Do not accept a pet that displays *any* signs of illness or poor condition. Such signs are: dull or weeping eyes, runny nose, forefeet that are wet or stained from constantly wiping the nose, lumps, swellings, abrasions, bald spots, and any sore areas. The tail should ideally be complete, not bitten off at the end. The anus should be clean and should not show signs of fecal staining resulting from diarrhea. The rat should not display any signs of breathing difficulty, such as wheezing. It should not have any problems moving around. It should not sit hunched up with its hair standing "off" its body when its cagemates are moving around without difficulty.

Most important, its teeth should be inspected to see that they just touch at their tips. If they are not correctly aligned so that the top teeth wear against the bottom ones (thus vice versa), your pet may experience great difficulty in eating.

→ These rat hobbyists let their pets get acquainted following a show. Rats as pets are becoming increasingly popular in a number of countries.

◆ Feeding rats is a relatively straightforward matter, as they will happily accept a wide variety of foods.

◆ A hooded rat having a snack. Note the well-developed claws, which enable the animal to easily pick up bits of food.

Feeding

Rats are omnivorous animals. This means that they will eat foods of both animal and plant origins. They are simple to feed because they are cosmopolitan in what they will accept, which is one reason why they have been able to survive so successfully. What you might eat, so will your pet rat. You can purchase any of the commercially prepared rodent (hamster, mouse, gerbil, or guinea pig) or rabbit mixtures, but make sure that the one that you select contains a variety of ingredients.

In non-packaged form, the following are just some of the examples of the foods you can feature in the diet of your pet: all grain foods, such as wheat, barley, crushed oats, bran, rice, and their like; breakfast cereals and other products derived from grain, such as bread, dog biscuits, and cookies (ration those that are sweetened); all popular seeds sold for caged birds, such as canary, millet, sunflower,

◆ Feeding fresh unprocessed foods will help to meet your pet's needs for vitamins and minerals.

safflower, hemp, linseed, unsalted peanuts and other nuts. Ration seeds such as hemp, sunflower, linseed, and peanuts, as they are very rich in proteins and fats.

Rats, like all other animals, exhibit preferences for certain foods; so it is best to offer your pet a range of vegetables and fruits to see which ones it likes. Some examples are carrots, green vegetables, apples, grapes, and wild plants, which should be thoroughly rinsed to remove any potentially dangerous chemicals that have been sprayed on them. Dairy products such as cheese, butter (on bread), and milk will be relished. Hard-boiled egg and milk-soaked bread will be greatly enjoyed. You can also offer bits of bacon, chicken, and other meats. Boiled fish will be eaten as well.

To keep your pet's teeth in good condition, you can feed slightly stale wholemeal bread—it is hard and provides something good for your pet to gnaw on. Fruit-tree branches will help in this matter as well.

The best feeding regimen will be based on one of the commercial mixes blended with a range of the fresh foods just discussed. This ensures a nicely balanced diet that lacks none of the important vitamins and minerals, and that is also very appetizing. Only if your rat's diet lacks plenty of variety will there be a need to offer vitamin supplements, and then only under veterinary advice. Excess of some vitamins can be as dangerous as a lack of them. Water must always be available to your pet on an ad lib basis. It should be replenished every day so that it is fresh and free from dust or fecal matter.

↞ Some food items will be more preferred than others. The only way to determine your pet's favorites is by offering a wide variety of foods.

↞ A gravity-fed water bottle is the ideal means of providing your rat with water. Photo courtesy Rolf C. Hagen Corp.

→ The rat in the foreground has just tipped over the food bowl. This is why food bowls should be of the crock variety.

→ Rats can be very discerning in their eating habits and often carefully sniff a food item before they consume it.

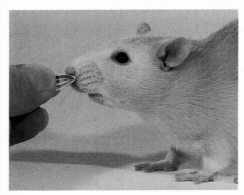

Feeding Containers

Any small dish can be used as a feed container, but the little earthenware pots made for small mammals and sold in your local pet shop are best. They are heavy and so are not easily tipped over. Purchase one for dry foods and one for fresh foods or damp mashes. Water is best supplied via a gravity-fed water bottle,

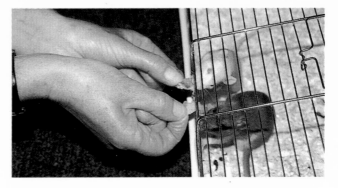

→ If your rat is well acclimated to you, it will run to the front of its cage when you approach, especially if you have a treat!

the type sold for hamsters, mice, rats, and other small pets. If your pet is a youngster, be sure it knows how to use the bottle. Until you actually see your pet use the bottle, it is best to also give him some water in a little earthenware dish.

The quantity of food and water that your rat will consume is, of course, an individual matter. By trial and error, you will soon know how much to give. Your pet should always have access to both dry foods and water. Only occasionally will you find an individual that will become obese because it eats more than it needs to. Most rats eat only what they need. Should your pet get too fat, simply reduce the quantity, never the quality, of the foods. Never withhold meals to slim your pet, as this could be dangerous to its health.

Breeding and Exhibiting

Although rats breed very freely, it is not advisable to get involved in this side of the hobby until you have gained some practical experience in their management. Apart from the potential problems that may come along, there is the fact that you just might end up with many more youngsters than you can find homes for. Your financial commitment to the hobby will go up quite a bit because you will need extra housing for the many youngsters that you will produce, the more so if you decide to retain one or two of them for further breeding.

Additionally, the more rats you keep the less time you will have to devote to any one individual. Overall, this means they are thought of less as pets and more as a hobby. If you plan to become an exhibitor, you may

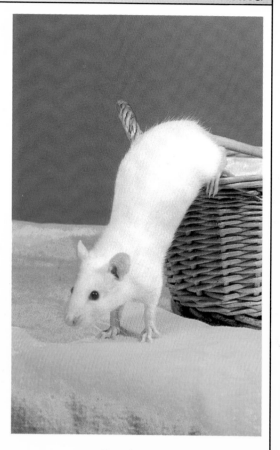

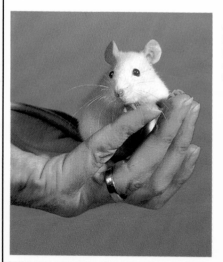

◀ A very docile pink-eyed white. Naturally, a rat may bite if it is handled incorrectly, but this is equally true of just about every other kind of pet.

► Rats that are not of show quality can still make very good pets.

► Rats develop very quickly, as you can see by this photo of a two-week-old rat and a two-day-old rat.

A litter of five-week-old rat youngsters. They were orphaned shortly after birth and had to be handreared, which is often not successful. They all survived and lived to the average age of two years.

An adult male rex rat. Note that even its whiskers are curled.

An average-sized rat litter. At birth, rats are blind and naked.

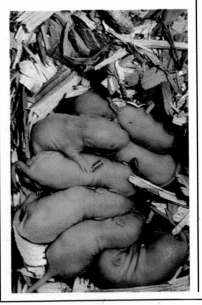

want to be a breeder because it is far more gratifying to exhibit rats that you have bred.

As a breeder, the object will not be to simply produce more rats. There is no shortage of these pets. You must strive to make quality your objective. Even then, many of the youngsters will not meet the required high standards of exhibition.

The Breeding Room

When you begin your breeding operations, it is best to conduct them in a spare room that you can devote to the hobby, or in an outdoor shed that can be carefully set up in a business-like manner. Day-to day-chores should be able to be attended to easily and in relative comfort. This means having water, sewerage, and electricity at your disposal.

A breeding room should be equipped with shelves so that the cages can be placed at convenient heights and easily moved around. Food should be stored in secure bins or similar containers because you do not want it contaminated by wild mice or rats. It is very important that the room be well ventilated (but not drafty). Lack of ventilation is the root cause of many problems related to the buildup of pathogenic organisms. The breeding room should be light and airy, but do remember that sunlight should not shine directly on the actual accommodations. The breeding room should also include an adequate work area in which routine tasks such as food preparation can be performed.

Cages and food/water containers should be numbered so that they are always kept together. You should have at least one or two spare cages or aquariums so that, on a rotation basis, all housing goes through a period when it has no residents and can be thoroughly cleaned and left empty.

Sexing Rats

Rats can be sexed as early as three to four weeks of age. Lift the rat bodily (not by the tail) in a gentle but secure manner so that you can inspect its anal area. The distance between the anus and the genitals is closer in females (does) than it is in males (bucks). Further, you should be able to see evidence of the male's testes in the

◆ This infant rat is being fed by means of a doll's baby bottle. Handrearing is difficult and time consuming, but seeing a youngster survive to maturity makes all of the effort worthwhile.

◀ A comparison of the sexes. With a little practice, young rats can be sexed quite easily.

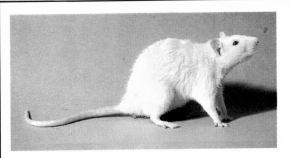

◄ A champagne rex rat.

◄ A Himalayan rat.

◆ A mother rat nursing her litter.

scrotal sac. The nipples of females are evident within weeks after birth, so the seller should be able to sex your pet without problems—but do double check yourself.

Breeding Strategy

Although rats can be bred on a colony system because they are gregarious in their social structure, this method is not recommended for the average hobbyist. It is known as uncontrolled breeding and is not the way for you to proceed. You need to have control over which females are mated to which males. You should pair your pets on the basis of their individual merits and on what they can pass on to their offspring.

Never overcompensate for features when selecting partners. For example, if one rat has a rather long back, do not pair it with one having a short back. Instead, select one that has an ideal length. This policy will ultimately result in reducing the genetic variation for back length in your stock, which is the goal that you want to achieve. The same approach applies to all other physical features.

Breeding Facts

Does are polyestrus, which means they have many breeding periods during each year. Spring, summer, and early fall are the best breeding times, although under artificial-light conditions these pets will readily breed year 'round. Although a doe can be sexually mature when as young as eight weeks old, you should not mate her until she is at least 12 or more weeks old. This allows her to reach physical maturity. The buck should be a little older. Always pair an unproven rat (either sex) to one with previous experience.

A doe may have anywhere up to 12 litters in a year. However, to breed a rat with such frequency is poor policy because it can only result in smaller and less vigorous offspring. It will deplete the doe of energy.

In rats, the estrus cycle (the time span between each estrus, or heat, period) is four to six days, and the actual estrus lasts about 20 hours. Place the female in the male's cage and see how they get on. If they fight, remove the female and wait until the next day to try the pair again. Repeat this procedure until the mating is successful.

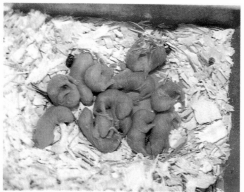

▲ This litter of rat kittens is just one day old.

The gestation period, meaning the time from mating to the births, is in the range of 21-26 days, and the litter size can be anything from 1-20. An average would be 8-11. The pups are born naked and blind but grow very rapidly. Their eyes are open before the 15th day (usually by the 12th), and by this time their fur has also grown in.

The pups leave the nest around the 22nd day, at which time they are weaned from their mother's milk. They will begin eating solid foods when only about 12 days of age—to coincide with the time their eyes are opening—when they can move around with ease. They can live together in a nursery house until about six to seven weeks of age, at which time they must be separated into sex groups so that the males do not start breeding and fighting.

▲ An inquisitive pink-eyed white. When breeding rats, select only animals that are sound and healthy.

The doe will have a postpartum estrus within 18 hours of delivering her litter, but

◆ Temperament is another important consideration when it comes to choosing breeding partners.

21

◄ This a show-quality rat. It has a nicely shaped head, and its ears are well spaced.

◄ This litter of rat babies is about six days old. Color markings are already visible. To be a successful breeder, you must first devise a good breeding plan. Additionally, you should plan beforehand what you will do with any youngsters that you may not wish to keep.

the gestation period will be longer if she is remated at this time. The embryos will not implant until some days later. Such repeat matings are not advisable.

Nest inspection is best done when the mother is out and feeding. Some young does may resent such inspection and devour their litter, but, in general, does are usually quite tolerant. Deformed offspring should be disposed of humanely.

Breeding Records

The keeping of exact breeding records is essential if you are to conduct anything other than a hit-or-miss program. The record cards should indicate the number of each parent of a mating, the date of mating, the birth date of the litter, the number born, and the number that survive. Note the sexes and their colors/patterns. Be very sure to record incidents of deformity, cannibalism, and whisker biting among the offspring (the ones with intact whiskers are usually the culprits). Like teeth misalignment, these problems are also thought to be hereditary, and it is essential that they be noted in your breeding records. *Never* breed any individual that is transmitting a problem. (If you keep good records, you will easily be able to determine which animals are not suitable for breeding.)

Exhibition

The show side of the rat hobby is run under the auspices of your national rat society, which may be in association with a mouse and/or hamster club, or run as an entity all its own.

The exhibits are judged against a written standard of excellence that allocates points for various features. Classes are organized for each sex and then for colors and patterns. The class winners then compete against each other in order to determine the group and sex winners, with the ultimate award of Best in Show.

Rats are exhibited in cages rather like the famous Maxey cage used for mice, but of a larger size. The cage must meet the requirements of the show society with regard to dimensions and exterior/interior paint used. It can carry no identifying marks so that the judge is not aware of who owns each of the exhibits.

◆ Rats being judged at a show in the UK. Regularly attending shows and closely observing other peoples' rats will help you to better assess the quality of your own rats.

◀ If you want to add new stock to your breeding lines, exhibitions are an excellent means by which you can do this.

Shows can range from small informal affairs at the local club level to the larger regional or national exhibitions, where the best rats in your country can be seen. In order to be a competitor, you need to join your national society, which will supply you with all of the needed information regarding this side of the hobby. Certainly, you will gain from visiting as many shows as you can before you decide if this side of the fancy appeals to you.

➤ A rat that is to be exhibited should be in tip-top condition. Preparing your rat for show actually begins long before the show day.

At the larger shows, you will be able to see what a quality rat looks like, and see all of the colors and patterns available. This would not otherwise be possible at a single location.

• If you are going to give your rat access to certain areas in your home, you must first be sure that all safety hazards have been eliminated. For example, a rat may gnaw on electrical wire, so it should be placed outside of your pet's reach.

• The more you know about your rat's normal behavior, the better able you will be to determine when the animal is not feeling well.

Health Care

Rats are quite hardy little animals and given proper care and nutrition should normally lead problem-free lives. But no animal is immune to diseases or injuries, so it all comes down to what sort of risks they are exposed to by their owners. Sound preventive husbandry is far better than treatment. This means careful attention to everyday chores.

Hygiene and Stress

Possibly the two areas of husbandry that are the most important are those relating to hygiene and stress. They are the main precursors of most diseases and conditions. Before we discuss them, it is important that you know each of your pets on an individual basis so that you can quickly spot when any one of them is not acting as it normally does. Often, behavioral traits may be the first signs, indeed the only signs, of a present or impending problem.

• Regular exercise can help to keep your rat in good physical condition.

▶ This black-eyed white rat has a large, but benign, tumor.

Signs to watch for are: disinterest in food or water, excessive sleeping, lack of interest in you, and difficulty in moving around. In a breeding room, an ill individual should immediately be placed in an isolation cage as far from the rest of the stock as possible. In the case of a pet, only you can determine if the condition warrants contacting the vet for advice. In any case, if there is no improvement within 36 hours, it would be wise to talk to your vet.

◆ This rat is almost three years old. Elderly and very young rats must be treated with extra special, gentle care.

◆ Toys like the one shown here are not advisable because a rat can ingest bits of the non-edible fiber and become ill.

◆ This healthy-looking rat is enjoying a small treat. Treats are fine, provided that they are fed in moderation.

HYGIENE:

Never underrate the importance of cleanliness. Clean all feeding vessels on a

◆ This rat and his Persian cat pal have known each other for a long time and regularly spend short periods of time together.

◆ *Never* put your rat's food directly on the bottom of the cage, as it will be contaminated by droppings. This is husbandry at its worst.

daily basis and do likewise to water containers at least every three days. Cracked or chipped food pots are best discarded, as the cracks can harbor bacteria. Cages should be cleaned each week, while soiled floor covering should be removed daily and not just covered over with more sawdust (or whatever substrate you use). Always wash your hands after handling each rat. Certainly do so after handling one that is ill, suspected of being so, or recovering from an illness. Routinely move cages so that you can clean underneath them and, of course, everywhere else in the case of a breeding room. Never feed foods that you suspect have been fouled, are damp, or are in any other way less than fresh. Be aware that you can easily transport bacteria into your

◆ Rats are relatively clean animals and do not require frequent bathing. When you do have to bathe your pet, do so in a draft-free area and make sure to carefully towel-dry him afterward.

▶ Rats are attractive and intelligent pets. This rat is enjoying the outdoors while resting securely in his owner's hand.

breeding room if you frequent places where there may be ill rats—such as pet shops, exhibitions, or the premises of friends who keep these pets. Wear a nylon overall while attending chores if you are a breeder.

STRESS:

This condition can be caused by a number of things. The more prevalent of them are as follows: overcrowding, bullying, excessive heat or cold, dampness, lack of adequate ventilation, poor handling, sudden frights on a regular basis (including the sudden switching on and off of lights when it is dark), and the nearness of possibly predatory animals, such as dogs, cats, or snakes. The remedy for each is obvious by its nature.

▲ This somewhat infirm and listless rat is very old. As is true for other kinds of pets, rats can be subject to a number of age-related health problems.

◀ A healthy rat will be alert and interested in its surroundings. It will have bright clear eyes and a clean dry nose.

◀ This rex rat developed an abscess, which had to be opened and drained. A scab is now forming over the affected area.

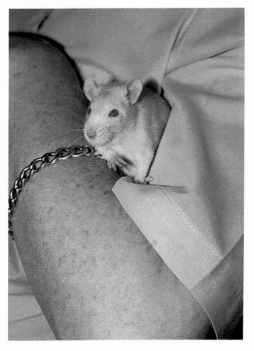

◆ Keeping your pet rat healthy is, for the most part, a matter of common sense.

◆ Like some other small rodents, rats will sometimes jump up onto their food bowls. There is no harm in this unless the animal accidentally used the bowl as a toilet.

Treatments

Once you are convinced that your pet is ill, you should immediately place its cage in a warm location, as this in itself may clear up minor chill-related problems. If the pet has diarrhea, this can indicate a whole range of problems, the more so if it is accompanied by other clinical signs. Make a note of them and how rapidly the problem has advanced, and then contact your vet without delay.

Do not attempt to administer antibiotics without veterinary advice. They can be extremely dangerous to rodents due to the adverse effect they may have on the pet's digestive system and its production of enzymes and vitamins. Rats are large enough to undergo injections without too much risk of shock, but your vet will counsel you on suggested treatments. Minor wounds caused by fighting should be carefully cleaned and treated with an antiseptic lotion or cream. The wound will usually heal up quickly, but keep your eyes on it until it does so. Deep lacerations should be treated by your vet.

Quarantine

The breeder should have isolation quarters for all newly acquired animals. This is very important because any individual that is incubating a disease can easily pass it to the rest of the stock once the disease manifests itself. The suggested isolation period is 14-21 days. During this time, you can routinely treat the newcomer for parasites such as fleas or lice, as well as satisfy yourself that it is eating well and generally maintaining good health.

Which Variety?

The body structure of all fancy rats is the same. There are no breeds, as in dogs and cats, just varieties produced by mutant genes that affect colors, patterns, and hair type. In hair type, there is the normal smooth-coated variety, and there is the rex. In the rex, the longer coarse guard hairs that provide waterproofing in the normal coat are shorter and somewhat softer. When rex rats are youngsters, the coat has a marcel-type wave. As they mature, the

⬤ As the popularity of the rat fancy has increased, so has the number of rat color varieties increased.

◀ An adult male chocolate rat.

◀ This rat is about to begin eating his meal, which is a blend of seeds, grains, and other healthful food items.

→ For some hobbyists, the potential for the development of new colors and patterns is one of the most exciting aspects of the rat fancy.

→ A number of pretty color varieties in the fancy rat have developed as a result of mutations.

coat becomes more open. This coat type is still far from perfected in this pet, so it does not compare with the velvet sheen of the rex rabbits. The rex coat can be combined with any of the colors and patterns because it is inherited independently. It is possible that one day we will see both the satin and the longhaired coat in rats, just as in mice.

Coat Colors

While the range of color shades is not yet as extensive as in mice, it is nonetheless wide enough to give you plenty of choices. The wild coloration in rats is known as agouti. This color pattern is a mixture of black, brown, and yellow hairs overlaid in such a way that it creates the ticked agouti effect. The underbelly fur is white to cream. In the fancy rat, the agouti is a more rich brown; but even so, it is not a popular color, no doubt because it reminds people of the wild rat.

A mutant gene has the effect of increasing the amount of black melanin deposited along the hair shaft. The result is that the brown, yellow, or cream-white areas of the hair become black. This produces the self black. The quality of black in rats is very variable and ranges from rather poor to quite nice—without reaching the same standard as seen in mice, rabbits, guinea pigs, or cats.

Another mutant gene reduces the black pigment to brown. The effect is to create cinnamon and chocolate colors. This is thus an agouti minus the black areas of the coat— creating a more overall brown with lighter ticking. The champagne color is a soft beige, created by what is called the pink-eyed dilution. This mutant gene reduces the depth of the brown to produce a more evenly colored rat with pink eyes.

By this recombination of mutations that have appeared over the years, and will continue to do so in the future, other colors, such as pearl, mink, and blue have been created. The white rat has always been a popular choice in the fancy, though it is more correctly called the albino. This is because it has red eyes. The albino is distinguished from a true white because of its red eyes. The "color" is created by yet another mutation that prevents the formation of any color pigments. The red of the eye is the hemoglobin of the blood, not a color pigment.

↟ Frontal close-up of a rat. Members of this species do not have very good vision, but they do have highly developed olfactory capabilities.

An albino still has all of the color genes in its genetic makeup, but they cannot express themselves because of the mutant gene. However, if an albino is paired to a colored rat, for example, a black, then all of the offspring will be black and will carry the albino gene in single dose. Only when the albino gene is in a double dose is it able to suppress color.

↟ A Siamese rat. Many pet shops stock fancy rats. If your pet shop dealer doesn't have the particular color variety that you are interested in, perhaps he can special order it for you.

Color Patterns

There are only two basic color patterns seen in rats, but one of them shows considerable variation in its expression. These patterns are as follows:

HIMALAYAN:

This pattern is similar to that seen in rabbits, guinea pigs, cats, and other pets. The head is

▲ T.F.H. Publications offers a number of other good books about rats, including the two shown here. These publications are available at pet shops.

▼ Part of the appeal of rats is the fact that they have simple needs. Good housing, a proper diet, and regular exercise will help to keep your pet healthy and content.

pigmented, as are the "points" (the ears, tail, and feet). The color of the points may be any color that is seen in the fancy. In an ideal specimen, the body color is white, or as near to it as possible. This pattern is thermo-sensitive, meaning that the hotter the environment the paler the color points become. The points tend to get darker as the individual gets older. Baby Himalayans are all white when they are born and display the pigmented points only as the days go by and their extremities (the points) cool down and allow pigment to form. If the body color is more of a cream brown than white, it is called Siamese.

WHITE SPOTTING:

This pattern is very variable, and the variations, which do not breed true like the self colors, are given different names. Each variation is, in fact, a colored rat that carries a given amount of white. At one end of the range there can be an almost black rat with just a few patches or spots of white. At the other extreme, there is what appears to be a white rat with just a few spots of black on it. When the color covers the head, the shoulders, and extends down the back as a progressively narrower stripe, it is known as hooded. If the color is restricted to the head only, it is called capped. If the white is restricted to just the underbelly, feet, and a spot on the forehead, it is called a Berkshire (for the English county). The Irish pattern is characterized by a white underbelly and a patch of white on the chest. Finally, there is the variegated rat, which displays a mixture of white and colored hairs on the body and has a white underbelly.